IRELAND 2016 HUMAN RIGHTS REPORT

EXECUTIVE SUMMARY

Ireland is a multiparty parliamentary democracy with an executive branch headed by a prime minister (Taoiseach), a bicameral parliament (Oireachtas), and a directly elected president. The country held free and fair parliamentary in February and presidential elections in 2011.

Civilian authorities maintained effective control over the security forces.

The principal human rights problems were discrimination against Traveller and Romani communities, sexual assault and domestic violence, and lengthy asylum determinations.

Other reported human rights problems included poor conditions in a few prisons; violence and discrimination against immigrants; gaps in women's reproductive health; and unequal pay and promotions for women in the workplace.

The government took steps to prosecute officials who committed human rights abuses, including in the security services and elsewhere in the government.

Section 1. Respect for the Integrity of the Person, Including Freedom from:

a. Arbitrary Deprivation of Life and other Unlawful or Politically Motivated Killings

There were no reports the government or its agents committed arbitrary or unlawful killings.

b. Disappearance

There were no reports of politically motivated disappearances.

c. Torture and Other Cruel, Inhuman, or Degrading Treatment or Punishment

The law prohibits such practices, and there were no reports government officials employed them.

In a November 2015 Council of Europe's Committee for the Prevent of Torture (CPT) report of its 2014 visit to the country, the CPT reported several allegations of police mistreatment, describing these as "mostly involving blows with batons, as well as slaps, kicks, and punches to various parts of the body." Most allegations involved incidents occurring at the time of arrest.

Prison and Detention Center Conditions

The majority of prisons met international standards, but some failed to meet prisoners' basic hygiene needs.

Physical Conditions: As of October 14, prisons had fewer inmates than the official capacity of the system, although some facilities, especially those for women, exceeded capacity. Food, potable water, heating, ventilation, lighting and medical care were adequate. In 2015 there were 22 reported deaths in the prison system.

At times authorities held detainees awaiting trial and detained immigrants in the same facilities as convicts. Authorities placed most juveniles in child-detention schools, but they held an average of 11 juveniles who were 17 years old in an adult prison at Wheatfield Place of Detention.

There were several incidents during the year at Oberstown Children's Detention Campus, the country's youth detention facility. Violence reportedly occurred frequently, with three breakouts reported in the first half of the year. Oberstown was understaffed with some personnel on sick leave due to incidents of violence committed against them. In August, Oberstown staff held an eight-hour work stoppage after they raised concerns about their workplace safety. During this work stoppage, detainees staged a rooftop demonstration and started a fire at the facility.

The inspector of prisons expressed concern that a minority of prison officers abused their authority by bullying, intimidating, acting to ensure the discomfiture of prisoners, and taking other measures to disparage prisoners under their control. There was also growing concern about prisoner-on-prisoner violence, with ethnic minorities especially vulnerable. In November 2015 the Office of the Inspector of Prisons, an independent statutory body, released an assessment of the prison service culture that highlighted negative elements within the penal system and the inability of prison leadership to take effective, positive, and corrective steps to address deficiencies.

Prisoners in some older facilities continued to lack sanitary facilities in their cells and had to use chamber pots in a practice known as "slopping out," which national and international humanitarian organizations referred to as inhuman treatment. On July 18, the minister for justice officiated at the opening of the new Cork prison, which had an official capacity of 296, with in-cell sanitation and improved facilities. On June 27, the Irish Prison Service initiated its Capital Strategy 2016-21 to renovate cells in Limerick and Portlaoise Prisons, which the service maintained would eliminate the "slopping out" practice. Human rights groups continued to criticize understaffing and poor working conditions at the Central Mental Health Hospital in Dundrum, the country's only secure mental health facility.

In its 2014 report, the CPT criticized conditions in a number of prisons. For example, at the Midlands Prison authorities separated certain inmates for their own protection, specifically to protect them against prison gangs or from aggressive behavior by other prisoners, and housed two to a cell in cells designed to hold one. The cells were in poor condition, with leaking sinks, broken windows, and no hot water. In the same prison, the CPT reported disorganized health services. In Limerick Prison, access to health care also seemed inadequate. The CPT indicated there appeared to be no clear legal basis or operating procedure for regulating prisoners in the equivalent of solitary confinement.

Administration: Recordkeeping on prisoners was generally adequate, but the Office of the Inspector of Prisons and nongovernmental organizations (NGOs) were critical of insufficient detail in the reporting. In his June 2015 report on deaths of prisoners in custody or on temporary release, the inspector of prisons stated in some instances no real management structure existed or was deficient, and staff did not follow standard operating procedures or adequately maintain proper records.

In its November 2015 report, the CPT noted Cloverhill Prison's lack of an automatic reporting obligation by prison doctors of prisoner injuries, which the CPT stated would help prevent abuse by prison officials.

Prisoners can submit complaints about their treatment to the prison service; the inspector of prisons has oversight of the complaints system. The Irish Human Rights and Equality Commission's (IHREC) Human Rights Committee expressed concern that complaint procedures did not provide for a fully independent system to deal with all serious complaints. An August report by the inspector of prisons said that while the overall complaints system was reliable, it was lacking in several areas due to the failure of employees to observe the agreed protocol, a lack of independent oversight, and a general absence of accountability. During the year the minister for justice accepted the inspector's recommendation that the Office of the Ombudsman be given a role to assure independent oversight.

Independent Monitoring: The Office of the Inspector of Prisons, an independent statutory body, conducted multiple inspections and independent reviews of detention facilities and methods. NGOs reported that the prison inspector function was effective.

The government permitted visits and monitoring by independent human rights observers and maintained an open invitation for visits from UN special rapporteurs.

Improvements: In a November 2015 report, the CPT noted both several allegations of mistreatment and the continued improvement in treatment of persons in national police (Garda) custody. The number of prisoners using chamber pots dropped from 1,003 to 85. In its 2015 report, the CPT noted steps authorities had taken since its 2010 visit to reduce overcrowding "significantly" by opening new facilities and reducing the number of persons detained in several others. The minister for justice and equality officially opened the new Cork Prison during the year.

d. Arbitrary Arrest or Detention

The constitution prohibits arbitrary arrest and detention, and the government generally observed these prohibitions.

Role of the Police and Security Apparatus

An Garda Siochana (Garda) is the national police force. It maintains internal security and is under the control of the Department of Justice and Equality. The defense forces are responsible for external security under the supervision of the Department of Defense but are also authorized certain domestic security responsibilities in support of the Garda.

Civilian authorities maintained effective control over the Garda and the army. Controversies related to the oversight of police, and particularly their treatment of whistleblowers, continued during the year. In 2015 the parliament enacted legislation allowing police officers to disclose allegations of wrongdoing within the police service to the Garda Siochana Ombudsman Commission (GSOC) on a confidential basis. By law the Garda ombudsman is responsible for conducting independent investigations, following referrals from the Garda in circumstances in which police conduct might have resulted in death or serious harm to a person. In 2015 the ombudsman initiated 52 such investigations, 15 of which involved fatalities. In February 2015 the parliament enacted legislation expanding the oversight powers of the GSOC. There were no reports of impunity involving the security forces.

In 2015 the GSOC received 1,996 complaints from the public, the most common of which involved investigations, arrests, road policing, customer service, and searches. The largest number of allegations against police related to abuse of authority or neglect of duty.

Arrest Procedures and Treatment of Detainees

An arrest typically requires a warrant issued by a judge, except in situations necessitating immediate action for the protection of the public. The law provides the right to a prompt judicial determination of the legality of a detention, and authorities respected this right. Authorities must inform detainees promptly of the charges against them and, with few exceptions, may not hold them longer than 24 hours without charge. For crimes involving firearms, explosives, or membership in an unlawful organization, a judge may extend detention for an additional 24 hours upon a police superintendent's request. The law permits detention without charge for up to seven days in cases involving suspicion of drug trafficking, although police must obtain a judge's approval to hold such a suspect longer than 48 hours. The law requires authorities to bring a detainee before a district court judge "as soon as possible" to determine bail status pending a hearing. A court may refuse bail to a person charged with a crime carrying a penalty of five years' imprisonment or longer, or when a judge deems continued detention necessary to prevent the commission of another offense.

The law permits detainees and prisoners, upon arrest, to have access to attorneys. The court appoints an attorney if a detainee does not have one. The law allows detainees prompt access to family members.

Detainee's Ability to Challenge Lawfulness of Detention before a Court: Persons arrested or detained are entitled to challenge in court the legal basis of their detention and obtain release if they have been found to be unlawfully detained.

<u>Protracted Detention of Rejected Asylum Seekers or Stateless Persons</u>: According to the CPT report of its 2014 visit, authorities held immigration detainees at Cloverhill Prison with detained and convicted prisoners where, in some cases, convicts bullied immigration detainees.

e. Denial of Fair Public Trial

The constitution provides for an independent judiciary, and the government generally respected judicial independence.

Trial Procedures

The law provides for the right to a fair public trial, and an independent judiciary generally enforced this right.

Defendants enjoy the right to the presumption of innocence, to be informed promptly and in detail of the charges against them, to be present at their trial, and to a fair and public trial except in certain cases. Defendants have the right to an attorney of their choice or one provided at public expense. They can confront witnesses and present their own testimony and evidence. Defendants have the right to adequate time and facilities to prepare a defense and to access government-held evidence. They have the right not to be compelled to testify or confess guilt. There is a right to appeal. The law extends the rights to all defendants.

The law provides for a nonjury Special Criminal Court (SCC) when the director of public prosecutions certifies a case to be beyond the capabilities of an ordinary court, such as terrorist or criminal gang offenses. A panel of three judges, usually including one High Court judge, one circuit judge, and one district judge, hears such cases. They reach their verdicts by majority vote. The Irish Council on Civil Liberties, Amnesty International, and the UN Human Rights Committee noted that authorities expanded the jurisdiction of the SCC in recent years to cover most offenses related to organized crime. They expressed concern that the SCC used a lower standard for evidence admissibility, and there was no appeal against a prosecuting authority's decision to send a case to the SCC. In October 2015 the justice minister announced the establishment of a second SCC with seven judges appointed during the year to try terrorist and gang-related offenses. The minister cited long delays in processing cases as a reason for the second court. The Irish Council for Civil Liberties and other national and international organizations criticized the move to expand the use of SCCs.

Political Prisoners and Detainees

There were no reports of political prisoners or detainees.

Civil Judicial Procedures and Remedies

An independent and impartial judicial system hears civil cases and appeals on civil matters, including damage claims resulting from human rights violations. Complainants may bring such claims before all appropriate courts, including the Supreme Court. Individuals may lodge a complaint (or application) with the European Court of Human Rights for alleged violations of the European Convention on Human Rights by the state if they have exhausted all available legal remedies in the Irish legal system, including an appeal to the Supreme Court.

f. Arbitrary or Unlawful Interference with Privacy, Family, Home, or Correspondence

The constitution prohibits such actions, and there were no reports that the government failed to respect these prohibitions.

Section 2. Respect for Civil Liberties, Including:

a. Freedom of Speech and Press

The law provides for freedom of speech and press, and the government respected these rights. An independent press, an effective judiciary, and a functioning democratic political system combined to promote freedom of speech and press.

Freedom of Speech and Expression: The law prohibits words or behaviors likely to generate hatred against persons, in the country or elsewhere, because of their race, nationality, religion, national origins, or sexual orientation. The law prohibits blasphemy, defined as publishing or uttering "matter that is grossly abusive or insulting in relation to matters held sacred by any religion, thereby causing outrage among a substantial number of the adherents of that religion." The law permits defendants to argue "genuine literary, artistic, political, scientific, or academic value" as a defense. There was only one prosecution for blasphemy since 1955 and none under the most recent (2009) law.

Press and Media Freedoms: The independent media were active and expressed a wide variety of views. The same prohibitions against language likely to generate hatred and blasphemy that affected freedom of speech also applied to the press. The government can prohibit the state-owned radio and television network from broadcasting any material "likely to promote or incite to crime or which would tend to undermine the authority of the state." Authorities did not invoke these prohibitions during the year.

Censorship or Content Restrictions: The Censorship of Publications Board has the authority to censor books and magazines deemed indecent or obscene. The board did not exercise this authority during the year. The Irish Film Classification Office must classify films and videos before they can be shown or distributed. It must cut or prohibit any film considered "indecent, obscene, or blasphemous" or which tends to "inculcate principles contrary to public morality or subversive of public morality." During the year the classification office did not prohibit any films or videos.

Internet Freedom

The government did not restrict or disrupt access to the internet or censor online content, and there were no credible reports that the government monitored private online communications without appropriate legal authority. Consistent with an EU directive, the government requires telecommunication companies to retain information on all telephone and internet contacts (not content) for two years. According to statistics of the International Telecommunication Union, approximately 81 percent of the population used the internet during the year.

Academic Freedom and Cultural Events

There were no government restrictions on academic freedom or cultural events.

b. Freedom of Peaceful Assembly and Association

The constitution provides for the freedoms of assembly and association, and the government generally respected these rights.

c. Freedom of Religion

See the Department of State's *International Religious Freedom Report* at www.state.gov/religiousfreedomreport/.

d. Freedom of Movement, Internally Displaced Persons, Protection of Refugees, and Stateless Persons

The constitution and law provide for freedom of internal movement, foreign travel, emigration, and repatriation, and the government generally respected these rights. The government cooperated with the Office of the UN High Commissioner for Refugees (UNHCR), the International Organization for Migration, and other humanitarian organizations in providing protection and assistance to refugees, asylum seekers, stateless persons, and other persons of concern.

Protection of Refugees

Access to Asylum: The law provides for the granting of asylum or refugee status, and the government established a system for providing protection to refugees. Asylum seekers whose initial applications are rejected can appeal the decision. Asylum seekers have access to legal advice.

NGOs and the UN Human Rights Committee expressed concern over the length and complexity of the application and appeal processes. In 2015 the average length of stay was 38 months. Almost 10 percent (450 of 4,696) of asylum seekers had been in the country for more than three years, awaiting decisions on their asylum applications or appeals. The commissioner of the Office of the Refugee Applications said the office had received 3,276 asylum applications in 2015, compared with 1,448 in 2014. There were 3,790 individuals removed or deported from the country in 2015, an increase from the 2,700 in 2014. The Refugee Appeals Tribunal indicated the number of cases reviewed in 2015 more than doubled with the tribunal hearing 799 cases, compared with 367 in 2014. It also issued rulings in 640 appeals--a 158 percent increase with 1,675 cases awaiting a decision.

Safe Country of Origin/Transit: The country generally follows the EU's Dublin III Regulation, which permits the return of asylum applicants to the EU member state of original entry for adjudication of asylum claims. In September 2015 the government agreed to participate in an EU decision to distribute 120,000 migrants and asylum seekers to various countries within the EU without regard to the Dublin III provisions. Until October 550 refugees and asylum seekers arrived in the country under the Irish Refugee Protection Program, with a further 1,300 scheduled to arrive in 2017.

Employment: Asylum applicants may not work.

<u>Access to Basic Services</u>: The country employs a system called "direct provision" that includes housing, meals, a weekly cash allowance, and access to health care for asylum seekers. Children have access to education. NGOs and the UN Human Rights Committee expressed concern about the effects of the direct provision system, specifically noting that the prolonged accommodation of asylum seekers (an average of five years and more than seven years for 20 percent of residents) was not conducive to family life and had detrimental effects on adults and children.

<u>Durable Solutions</u>: In 2015 the government operated a resettlement program accommodating up to 200 persons referred by UNHCR or identified through selection missions to UNHCR refugee operations.

<u>Temporary Protection</u>: The government also provided temporary protection (subsidiary protection) to individuals who may not qualify as refugees and, according to Eurostat, granted such protection to 375 persons during the year. Such individuals were entitled to temporary residence permits, travel documents, access to employment, health care, and housing. The country did not make determinations on subsidiary protection status at the same time as asylum status. This caused delays, as a separate subsidiary protection determination could take from several months to more than a year to complete.

Section 3. Freedom to Participate in the Political Process

The constitution provides citizens the ability to choose their government in free and fair periodic elections held by secret ballot and based on universal and equal suffrage.

Elections and Political Participation

<u>Recent Elections</u>: Observers reported the 2016 parliamentary and 2011 presidential elections were free and fair.

<u>Participation of Women and Minorities</u>: No law prevents women or members of minorities from voting or participating in the electoral process, and women and minorities did participate.

Section 4. Corruption and Lack of Transparency in Government

The law provides criminal penalties for corruption by officials, and the government generally implemented the laws effectively.

Corruption: There were no reports of government corruption during the year.

Financial Disclosure: Elected and appointed officials, as well as civil servants at the higher grades, are required to furnish a statement, in writing, to the Standards in Public Office Commission of their interests, the interests of their spouse, civil partner, or child that could materially influence the person in the performance of official functions. The commission verifies the disclosures. The financial disclosures of elected officials were made public. There are criminal and administrative sanctions for noncompliance.

Public Access to Information: The law provides for public access to government information and requires government agencies to publish information on their activities and make such information available to citizens, noncitizens, and foreign media upon request. Authorities generally granted freedom of information requests and provided mechanisms for appealing denials.

Legislation was enacted in 2014 extending the public's right to government information from all public bodies unless specifically exempt, in whole or in part, and from nonpublic bodies that are significantly funded by the state. The Garda, the National Treasury Management Agency Group, the Central Bank of Ireland, the industrial relations bodies, the Insolvency Service of Ireland, and the various ombudsmen enjoyed partial exemption from these requirements on grounds that release of certain information would affect their ability to perform core functions, or impact the interests of the security or the financial position of the country.

Section 5. Governmental Attitude Regarding International and Nongovernmental Investigation of Alleged Violations of Human Rights

A number of domestic and international human rights groups operated without government restriction, investigating and publishing their findings on human rights cases. Government officials often were cooperative and responsive to their views.

Government Human Rights Bodies: The law obliges public bodies to take account of human rights and equality in the course of their work. The IHREC, an independent organization, monitored adherence of public bodies to these legal obligations. The IHREC was active throughout the year, holding consultations, trainings, briefings, and policy reviews on a number of human rights issues. There is a human rights subcommittee of the parliamentary Committee on Justice, Defense, and Equality. Its role was to examine how issues, themes, and proposals before the parliament take into account human rights concerns.

Section 6. Discrimination, Societal Abuses, and Trafficking in Persons

Women

Rape and Domestic Violence: The law criminalizes rape, including spousal rape, and the government enforced the law. Most persons convicted received prison sentences of five to 12 years. According to the most recent report of director of public prosecution, in 2014 there were 82 prosecutions for sexual offenses, with an 89 percent conviction rate. The law criminalizes domestic violence. It authorizes prosecution of a violent family member and provides victims with "safety orders," which prohibit a person from engaging in violent actions or threats, and "barring orders," (restraining order) which prohibit an offender from entering the family home for up to three years. Anyone found guilty of violating a barring or protection order may receive a fine of up to 4,000 euros ($4,400), a prison sentence of 12 months, or both. The law covers cohabiting couples, including same-sex couples and parents with a child in common, but not individuals in intimate relationships who have not cohabited. Advocates criticized the government for the lengthy waiting periods necessary to obtain barring orders, including interim barring orders.

The government permitted domestic violence to be included among factors affecting child custody decisions.

The November 2015 EU Victims Directive commits the government to undertake key actions but was pending formal enactment into law. Criminal justice agencies began providing some services to victims to comply with the directive.

On January 20, Deputy Prime Minister (Tanaiste) and Minister for Justice and Equality Frances Fitzgerald initiated the *Second National Strategy on Domestic, Sexual, and Gender-based Violence 2016-2021*, an action plan that focuses on prevention of violence, services to victims, and data gathering. In November the deputy prime minister and the National Office for the Prevention of Domestic, Sexual, and Gender-Based Violence launched the national awareness campaign "What would you do?" The awareness campaign was a part of the second national strategy, and the government secured 950,000 euros ($1,006,000) to fund the campaign due to run from 2016 to 2021 to inform and change attitudes and educate the public about domestic violence.

Lack of data made it difficult to analyze the scale of domestic abuse and sexual violence in the country. In a 2014 report, the EU Agency for Fundamental Rights estimated that 26 percent of Irish women had experienced physical and/or sexual violence since the age of 15. According to the NGO Safe Ireland, domestic violence support services answered 48,888 helpline calls in 2014.

A 2014 Garda Inspectorate review found that police did not always correctly record domestic violence cases. While the police have a domestic violence policy in place, there was little evidence that it was effectively implemented. The inspectorate also found an inconsistent approach to dealing with victims, with some Garda displaying negative attitudes towards domestic violence by referring to calls as "problematic, time consuming, and a waste of resources." In 2015 the Garda commissioner established the Garda National Protective Services Bureau with specially trained officers to deal with sex crimes, domestic violence, and trafficking in persons who were also to provide guidance and assistance to police throughout the country.

NGOs expressed continued concern that funding levels, which had been cut during austerity and not fully restored, would limit support services for victims of family violence. They were also concerned about the lack of a mechanism to provide safe living quarters for migrant women experiencing domestic violence.

Female Genital Mutilation/Cutting (FGM/C): The law prohibits FGM/C for women and girls. The maximum penalty for performing FGM/C in the country or taking a girl to another country to undergo the procedure is a fine of up to 10,000 euros ($11,000), imprisonment for up to 14 years, or both. During the year Garda investigated a possible case of FGM of a young girl and arrested a man in Dublin for questioning. Police and other government authorities, as well as NGOs, were on heightened alert during school holidays. Teachers began receiving training in detecting signs that a child was in danger of FGM/C and were legally obligated to report such instances to police or child protection services.

Sexual Harassment: The law obliges employers to prevent sexual harassment and prohibits employers from dismissing an employee for making a complaint of sexual harassment. Authorities effectively enforced the law when sexual harassment was reported. The penalties can include an order requiring equal treatment in the future, as well as compensation for the victim up to a maximum of two years' pay or 40,000 euros ($44,000), whichever was greater. The law prohibits harassment and sexual harassment not only in employment but also in the supply of, and access to, goods and services.

Reproductive Rights: Couples and individuals have the right to decide the number, spacing, and timing of their children; manage their reproductive health; and have the information and means to do so, free from discrimination, coercion, and violence. The constitution gives equal status to the mother and the unborn child. In 2013 the country enacted the Protection of Life during Pregnancy Act to permit abortion in limited circumstances such as real and substantive risk to the life of the pregnant women. Some international and national organizations raised concerns about the lack of legal and medical clarity in implementing the act. Under the act procuring or assisting with an abortion in the country is a criminal offense with a maximum penalty of 14 years' imprisonment, although the statute had not been used. The IHREC highlighted concerns that the law disproportionately penalizes poor women, female asylum seekers, and undocumented migrants because they were unable to travel abroad to obtain an abortion. The Irish Family Planning Association expressed concerns with barriers stemming from fear of prosecution, which could decrease access to emergency health care services to deal with complications arising from abortions.

In June the UN Human Rights Committee found that a woman who had to choose between carrying a fatally ill fetus to term or seeking an abortion abroad was subjected to discrimination and cruel, inhuman, or degrading treatment as a result of the country's legal prohibitions on abortion.

Discrimination: The law provides women the same legal status and rights as men. Inequalities in pay and promotions, although prohibited by law, persisted in both the public and private sectors.

Children

Birth Registration: A person born after 2004 on the island of Ireland (including Northern Ireland) is automatically a citizen if at least one parent was an Irish citizen, a British citizen, a resident of either Ireland or Northern Ireland entitled to reside in either without time limit, or a legal resident of Ireland or Northern Ireland for three of the four years preceding the child's birth (excluding time spent as a student or an asylum seeker). Authorities register births immediately.

<u>Child Abuse</u>: The law criminalizes engaging in, or attempting to engage in, a sexual act with a child younger than 17. The maximum sentence in such cases is five years in prison, which can increase to 10 years if the accused is a person in authority, such as a parent or teacher. The law additionally proscribes any person from engaging in, or attempting to engage in, a sexual act with a juvenile younger than 15; the maximum sentence is life imprisonment. Tusla, the Child and Family Agency, provided child protection, early intervention, and family support services. The government also provided funding to NGOs that carried out information campaigns against child abuse as well as those who provided support services to victims.

<u>Early and Forced Marriage</u>: The legal minimum age for marriage is 18 years. Persons under 18 must obtain the permission of the Circuit Family Court or the High Court to marry.

<u>Female Genital Mutilation/Cutting (FGM/C)</u>: See information in women's section above.

<u>Sexual Exploitation of Children</u>: The law prohibits the commercial sexual exploitation of children and child pornography, and authorities enforced the law. Conviction of trafficking in children and taking a child from home for sexual exploitation carries a maximum penalty of life imprisonment. A person convicted of meeting a child for the purpose of sexual exploitation faces a maximum penalty of 14 years' imprisonment. The minimum age of consensual sex is 17.

The law provides for a fine of up to 31,000 euros ($34,100), a prison sentence of up to 14 years, or both for a person convicted of allowing a child to be used for pornography. For producing, distributing, printing, or publishing child pornography, the maximum penalty is 1,900 euros ($2,100), 12 months' imprisonment, or both. The Irish Society for the Prevention of Cruelty to Children criticized these penalties as too lenient.

<u>International Child Abductions</u>: The country is a party to the 1980 Hague Convention on the Civil Aspects of International Child Abduction. See the Department of State's *Annual Report on International Parental Child Abduction* at travel.state.gov/content/childabduction/en/legal/compliance.html.

Anti-Semitism

According to the 2011 census, the Jewish community numbered 1,984 persons. In November there were media reports of a man facing charges of making threats to kill or cause serious harm. During an incident the man made anti-Semitic threats and behaved erratically.

On January 24, the Holocaust Education Trust Ireland in association with the Department of Justice and Equality, the Office for the Promotion of Migrant Integration, and Dublin City Council organized a national Holocaust Day Memorial commemoration in which the prime minister, the foreign minister, other senior government ministers, and key public figures participated.

Trafficking in Persons

See the Department of State's *Trafficking in Persons Report* at www.state.gov/j/tip/rls/tiprpt/.

Persons with Disabilities

The law prohibits discrimination against persons with physical, sensory, intellectual, and mental disabilities in employment, education, air travel and other transportation, access to health care, the judicial system, or the provision of other state services. The government effectively enforced these provisions and implemented laws and programs to give persons with disabilities access to buildings, information, and communications. The National Disability Authority is the independent state agency responsible for setting and implementing disability standards, as well as directing disability policy. At the end of 2015, the prime minister launched the *Comprehensive Employment Strategy for People with Disabilities 2015-2024*, which established a minister of state for disability issues, a junior ministerial role, within the Departments of Social Protection, Justice and Equality, and Health.

There were instances of employment discrimination against persons with disabilities. Children with disabilities generally had full access to educational options at all levels. In a practice condemned by children's rights and mental health groups, authorities continued to admit minors to adult psychiatric units, with 95 reported admissions of children to adult units, according to the 2015 annual report of the Mental Health Commission. In July RTE (the state broadcaster) Investigations Unit uncovered failings in care services for the intellectually disabled. An unpublished 2013 internal Health Service Executive report leaked to

RTE Investigates suggested that the state's care services had repeatedly failed hundreds of adults with intellectual disabilities.

National/Racial/Ethnic Minorities

The law prohibits discrimination based on race, which includes color, nationality, ethnicity, and national origins, and the government enforced the law. Nevertheless, societal discrimination and violence against immigrants and racial and ethnic minorities remained a problem. The country's African population and Muslim community in particular experienced racially motivated physical violence, intimidation, graffiti, and verbal slurs. According to the Immigrant Council of Ireland (ICI), the number of reported racist incidents rose by 11 percent in 2015 to 240. NGOs reported that immigrants, particularly those of African descent, experienced unemployment disproportionately during the economic downturn.

During the year the ICI, the National Transport Authority, and nationwide public transport providers launched the #StopRacism campaign, celebrating diversity and encouraging witnesses to report racist incidents. The national police supported the campaign, as did the specialized Garda Racial and Intercultural Office dedicated to working with victims of racist incidents.

According to the 2011 census, 29,495 persons identified themselves as members of an indigenous group known as Travellers, with a distinct history and culture; however, the government does not officially recognize them as a distinct ethnic group. Irish Human Rights and Equality Commission's Chief Commissioner Emily Logan raised concerns over the lack of progress on Traveller ethnicity recognition since the country's first UN Universal Period Review in 2011. Despite antidiscrimination laws, Travellers continued to face societal discrimination and denial of access to education, employment, housing, sanitation, and basic services. Life expectancy for Traveller men was approximately 15 years less and for Traveller women 11.5 years less than that of the general population. The advocacy group Pavee Point criticized the Department of Health for not having convened the National Traveller Health Advisory Committee since 2012.

Advocacy groups criticized reductions in the Traveller accommodation budget, which was cut by 90 percent between 2008 and 2015. The law obliges local officials to develop suitable accommodation sites for Travellers and to solicit Traveller input. Traveller NGOs asserted many communities provided Travellers with housing that was unsuitable for their nomadic lifestyle or provided transient caravan camping sites that were unsafe and lacking basic services such as sanitary facilities, electricity, and water. Pavee Point criticized the absence of an agency to address the urgent need for improvements in housing and the implementation of existing policies in health, education, and employment.

During the year the Council of Europe's Committee of Social Rights determined that the country's law and practice violated the human rights of Travellers on the following grounds: inadequate conditions at many Traveller sites; insufficient provision of accommodation for Travellers; inadequate legal safeguards for Travellers threatened with eviction; and evictions carried out without necessary safeguards.

There was little data on Roma living in the country. The Irish census identifies persons by their nationality, not ethnicity, splitting Roma into national categories such as Slovakian, Romanian, or Hungarian. Pavee Point estimated that approximately 5,000 Roma lived in the country. Many Roma in the country cited discrimination in access to education, health services, housing, and employment. NGOs were critical of the Habitual Residence Condition, saying it was an obstacle for Roma to access social protection and services. NGOs also claimed Roma experienced prejudice, discrimination, and negative stereotyping.

Acts of Violence, Discrimination, and Other Abuses Based on Sexual Orientation and Gender Identity

The law prohibits discrimination based on sexual orientation with respect to employment, goods, services, and education. The law does not include gender identity as an explicit category, but the courts interpreted it as prohibiting discrimination against transgender persons.

A 2015 law made same sex marriage legal in the country. Also in 2015 the country established a process for enabling transgender individuals to achieve full legal recognition of their preferred gender and allow them to acquire a new birth certificate reflecting this change. Individuals older than 18 can self-declare, while 16- and 17-year olds can also apply for legal recognition based on their preferred gender.

The 1989 Incitement to Hatred Act is the country's legislation to combat incidents of hate speech. Civil liberties and civil society organizations criticized its effectiveness on the grounds that no specific legislation existed to deal with other forms of hate crimes or to ensure that prejudice was taken into account as an aggravating factor when sentencing criminals.

In July a group assaulted a man and subjected him to verbal homophobic abuse. The victim made a formal complaint to the Garda Siochana Ombudsman Commission concerning the way investigating officers treated him and his case. He alleged undue delays by the police, demeaning questions from the investigating officers, and a failure to secure his personal data in written correspondence.

Section 7. Worker Rights

a. Freedom of Association and the Right to Collective Bargaining

The constitution provides for the rights of workers to form and join independent unions, bargain collectively, and conduct legal strikes, and the government respected these rights. The law prohibits antiunion discrimination and provides for reinstatement of workers fired for union activity. All workers, regardless of occupation, have the right to freedom of association. The Industrial Relations (Amendment) Act 2015 reintroduced a mechanism for the registration of employment agreements between employers and trade unions governing wages and employment conditions.

Police and military personnel may form associations, technically not unions, to represent them in matters of pay, working conditions, and general welfare. The law does not require employers to engage in collective bargaining. The law provides for the right to strike, except for police and military personnel, in both the public and private sectors. Labor unions have the right to pursue collective bargaining and in most instances did so freely, with employers' cooperation in most cases. While workers are constitutionally protected in forming trade unions, employers are not legally obliged to recognize unions or to negotiate with them. The government facilitates freedom of association and trade union activity through the Labor Relations Commission, which promotes the development and improvement of industrial relations policies, procedures, and practices, and the Labor Court, which provides resolution of industrial relations disputes.

The government enforced laws protecting the right to freedom of association; there were no reports of violations of the law. The country allocated adequate resources to the government to provide oversight of labor relations. The Labor Court is a court of last resort for trade unions and employers and sought to process cases with a minimum of delay.

Workers freely exercised these rights. Unions conducted their activities without government interference. There were no reports of antiunion discrimination. Labor leaders did not report any threats or violence from employers.

During the year there were bus and rail strikes and stoppages by staff represented by the National Bus and Rail Union (NBRU) and the Services, Industrial, Professional and Technical Union (SIPTU). Dublin bus drivers picketed for four days as unions sought a 15 percent pay increase over three years for drivers and a 6 percent raise agreed in 2009 but subsequently deferred. Earlier in the year, unions rejected a Labor Court-recommended 8.25 percent increase. Unions suspended further strikes pending a vote by staff, after talks between management and unions at the Workplace Relations Commission in September. The deal would see Dublin bus staff receive pay raises totaling 11.25 percent over three years. In May the NBRU and SIPTU resolved a dispute with Irish Rail at the Workplace Relations Commission over issues including the restoration of pay cuts and claim for further increases.

b. Prohibition of Forced or Compulsory Labor

The law prohibits all forms of forced or compulsory labor, but there were reports of forced labor in the country. The government effectively enforced the law, but no labor traffickers were convicted during the year.

The Workplace Relations Commission (WRC) monitors compliance with employment rights, inspects workplaces, and has prosecution services aimed at enforcement of employment rights legislation.

The law considers forced labor to be human trafficking. The penalty for human trafficking is up to life imprisonment and an unlimited fine. These penalties were sufficient to deter violations. NGOs alleged employers subjected men and women to forced labor in construction, restaurant work, commercial fishing, car washes, and agriculture, as well as in private homes as domestic servants. The victims of forced labor were usually immigrants, either regular or undocumented.

The law allows undocumented workers to sue exploitative employers for back wages and compensation in cases of forced or compulsory labor. Trade unions and NGOs contended more needed to be done to identify and support victims and prosecute employers.

Also see the Department of State's *Trafficking in Persons Report* at www.state.gov/j/tip/rls/tiprpt/.

c. Prohibition of Child Labor and Minimum Age for Employment

The law prohibits employment of children under the age of 16 in full-time jobs. Employers may hire children who are 14 to 15 years old for light work on school holidays as part of an approved work experience or educational program. Employers may hire children older than 15 on a part-time basis during the school year. The law establishes rest intervals and maximum working hours, prohibits the employment of children 18 and younger for late-night work, and requires employers to keep detailed records of workers who are under 18. The law identifies hazardous occupations and occupational safety and health restrictions for workers under 18, which generally involve working with hazardous materials or chemicals. Employers must verify there is no significant risk to the safety and health of young people and take into account the increased risk arising from the lack of maturity and experience in identifying risks to their own safety and health. The law stipulates that exposure to physical, biological, and chemical agents or certain processes be avoided and provides a nonexhaustive list of agents, processes, and types of work from which anyone under 18 may require protection. The government effectively enforced applicable laws, and there were no reports that child labor occurred.

The WRC is responsible for enforcement, and it was generally effective, with adequate resources and investigative and enforcement powers. Employers found guilty of an offense are liable to a fine of up to 2,000 euros ($2,200). Continuing breaches of the act can result in a fine of up to 300 euros ($330) per day. The Health and Safety Authority has responsibility for overseeing hazardous occupations and can impose the same penalties as specified for other workers.

d. Discrimination with Respect to Employment and Occupation

The law bans discrimination in a wide range of employment and employment-related areas. It defines discrimination as treating one person in a less favorable way than another person based on color, political opinion, national origin, citizenship, social origin, language, sex; civil status; family status; sexual orientation; religion; age; disability, including physical, intellectual, learning, cognitive, or emotional disability; HIV-positive status or other communicable diseases and a range of other medical conditions; race and membership in the

Traveller community (also see section 6). The law specifically requires equal pay for equal work or work of equal value.

The Employment Equality Act 2015 eliminated certain exemptions for state-affiliated institutions. Members of the LGBTI community, divorcees, and single parents working in state-owned or state-funded schools and hospitals operated under religious patronage have the same legal protections against discrimination as workers in the private sector.

The law provides that employers are not required to continue an employee's employment if the employee in question is not capable of doing the job that he or she was employed to do. Discrimination persisted, but the government has mechanisms to combat the problem.

The government effectively enforced applicable laws, and the nature of penalties for violations was sufficient to deter violations. In January an Equality Tribunal awarded a teacher more than 65,000 euros ($68,900) in compensation after it concluded that she had been discriminated against by her school. The school was found to have discriminated against the teacher on grounds of her gender and by not taking reasonable steps to prevent or reverse her sexual harassment by a male employee of the school over a three-year period. A High Court judgment in February found that in a disability case employers must show that they had considered the redistribution of the employee's tasks to provide reasonable accommodation.

e. Acceptable Conditions of Work

The national minimum hourly wage was 9.15 euros ($10.06). Laws establishing and regulating wage levels cover migrant workers. The standard workweek is 39 hours. There are nine public holidays each year, to which full-time workers have immediate entitlement; part-time workers have entitlement when they have worked a total of 40 hours in the previous five weeks. Depending on the hours worked, employees are entitled to paid annual leave. Employees who work at least 1,365 hours are entitled to four weeks of leave but less time if they work less. The law also makes provisions for parental and maternity leave, caregiver's leave, and adoptive leave. The Paternity Leave and Benefit Act of 2016, which introduced statutory paternity leave of two weeks, went into effect on September 1. The law limits work in the industrial sector to nine hours per day and 48 hours per week. The law limits overtime work to two hours per day, 12 hours per week, and 240 hours per year. The government effectively enforced these standards. Although there is no statutory entitlement to premium pay for overtime, it could be arranged between employer and employee. The government sets occupational health and safety standards. The Low Pay Commission's second *Report to Government, Recommendations on the National Minimum Wage for 2016*, published in July recommended that the national minimum wage be increased by 1.1 percent to 9.25 euros ($10.18) per hour.

The Department of Jobs, Enterprise, and Innovation is responsible for enforcing occupational safety laws, and these laws provided adequate and comprehensive protection. Depending on the seriousness of the violation, courts may impose fines, prison sentences, or both for violating the law. The maximum penalty is three million euros ($3.3 million), imprisonment for up to two years, or both. The law also provides for immediate fines of up to 1,000 euros ($1,100) for certain offenses. There were no complaints from either labor or management during the year regarding shortcomings in enforcement. The government revamped its institutions responsible for regulating the workplace in 2015, merging five organizations into two. The new workplace relations system is composed of the Workplace Relations Commission, which deals with complaints, and the Labor Court, which has responsibility for appeals. The responsibilities of the Labor Relations Commission, National Employment Rights Authority, Equality Tribunal, Employment Appeals Tribunal, and Labor Court were merged into the two new bodies.

Allegations persisted that employers at times paid foreign migrant workers less than the minimum wage, particularly in the agricultural and construction sectors.

The informal economy was small, and although largely undocumented, was likely concentrated in the agricultural and services sectors.

Minimum wage, hours of work, and health and safety standards were effectively enforced in all sectors, including the informal economy. The WRC secures compliance with employment rights legislation through inspection and prosecution service. The WRC's Inspection Services have the power to carry out employment rights compliance inspections under employment legislation. Under the Workplace Relations Act 2015, the WRC has the power under a number of employment laws to bring summary prosecutions against employers who are alleged to be in breach of the law.

By law an employer may not penalize through dismissal, disciplinary action, or less favorable treatment employees who make a complaint or exercise their rights under health and safety legislation. Employers have an obligation to protect an employee's safety, health, and welfare at work as far as is reasonably practicable. There were 31 workplace fatalities as of October 3, many of them the result of farming accidents. Workers can remove themselves from situations that endanger health or safety without jeopardy to their employment.

www.ingramcontent.com/pod-product-compliance
Lightning Source LLC
Chambersburg PA
CBHW081259250726
48654CB00012B/1664